Blessings

Ginette Danis

BookLeaf
Publishing

Presentation by *BookLeaf Publishing*

Web: www.bookleafpub.com

E-mail: info@bookleafpub.com

ISBN: 978-93-95950-06-0

First edition 2022

DEDICATION

This book is dedicated to my husband Roch who has supported all of my dreams. Through both good and rough times, you have stood by my side.

ACKNOWLEDGEMENT

I would like to thank my precious husband Roch for supporting me in everything I decide to do. My children for believing their mother can accomplish this dream. And my precious family and friends for encouraging and supporting me also. I have been blessed throughout my journey with such amazing people.

PREFACE

I've always wanted to see my poems published in a book. It's been a dream of mine for so long but I've always hesitated since I didn't think my writing was good enough. This past year has been very difficult and has shown me that we never know what will happen. This opportunity presented itself and I decided to take it. Whatever happens I am happy I am doing this.

Greatest Gifts

The greatest gifts you can give to somebody;
Are your love, time, support and accepting them
completely.
Sharing laughter during those happy moments;
Wiping tears and listening when you want to
vent.

See not everyone will understand these special
bonds.
Some will judge you when you are not around.
Others will pretend they truly love you;
But will criticize every word or action that you
do.

By such amazing love I am surrounded;
To have amazing family and friends I feel
blessed.
Knowing that at time when I am feeling lost and
emotionally drained;
I know I have amazing support to lean on even
after I am fully charged.

As with any existing relationship;
You must treasure these family bonds and
friendships.

How or why your bonds have started doesn't matter;
What does is that you cherish them and treat them like a treasure.

Enjoy all those moments you share together.
Share messages, calls filled with tears and laughter.
Together make those special new memories;
And make sure they know you love them completely.

Give those hugs that show they are truly loved.
That give them a wonderful feeling by which a long time they will be surrounded.
Tell them "I love you" sincerely and regularly;
Those are the greatest gifts you can give to somebody.

Treasure

What may appear unimportant and unusual to
anyone;
Could be a treasure and priceless to someone.
What could appear like a small and simple act
you appear to be doig;
Has meant the world to the person who felt
themselves completely draining.

This journey we are at the moment traveling;
Is stressful and of our energy very demanding.
Add those events that are happening to us
personally;
Staying positive and happy is not easy for
anybody.

Things that are important for any time of this
journey;
Are support, love, friends and family.
And even though we are not in the same way
these times experiencing;
We must remember that together we can conquer
anyting.

So reach out to all your loved ones;
Bring love in your own special way to someone.

I can tell personally;
That gives you a feeling of being loved
completely.

Dear friends and family;
Let me start your days by sending hugs and love
from me.

Thankful

Everyone knows that I express my feelings
through my writing;
And that's how I do my best sharing.
But this time there is quite a bit of hesitation;
Cause I didn't want to share this situation.

But I was asked by someone to do so;
So I can let everyone know;
Whatever is happening to you personally;
You are not alone and it can happen to anybody.

The last few months have brought so many
events unfortunately;
That make me understand fully;
That we never know what life has in store for
anyone;
And that we should always cherish our loved
ones.

I am thankful every day;
For that person who decided to say;
Let's look further into this;
Because there is something there I don't want to
miss.

I am thankful every day;
To be surrounded by amazing people who love
me in their own way.
Who understand I'm currently going through a
different journey;
And are there to help me adapt and support me
fully.

I understand that every day;
There is someone whose life is affected in a very
shocking way.
Yet still they wake up every morning;
And will find at least one reason in their day to
be smiling.

Now don't get me wrong I'm not saying it's easy;
And I know it's true for everybody.
One considerate act you can do for everyone;
Is to remember and understand that they could
have signs that are not physically shown.

To everyone who in some way or another are
experiencing;
Events that are both physically and emotionally
draining.
I do hope you are by love, family and friends
surrounded;
And let me start by sending you love and hugs to
use when you feel drained.

Rough patches

To all my dear friends and family;
This past year has been really rough for
everybody.
A lot of things have happened that have left us
drained either physically or emotionally;
A lot of things are happening that we still don't
understand unfortunately.

We've learned that we all make mistakes;
Despite whatever decisions we make.
We will have our disagreements;
Since we are all different individuals with
different feeling and sentiements.

Life this year has thrown me a curve health wise
suddenly;
Yes there are days I am wondering why this is
happening to me.
But the support of you my dear friends and
family;
During these time have been a precious gift to
me.

So as the new year is fast approaching;

I want to say thank you and love to all of you I
am sending.
And remember that the most precious gift given
to all of you is family;
And to take every moment you can to say I love
you daily.

I hope the new year brings you all of you lots of
love, happiness and new memories.

Lives are like quilts

Our lives are like quilts in unique ways;
Each section represents for us special days.
Some memories we treasure in our hearts dearly;
And others we put in the back cause to thing of
them hurts deeply.

Our quilt also is create with the help of our
friends and family.
What we share with them is cherished deeply.
To this amazing creation that holds both good
and bad memories;
They hold their own place in our hearts, minds
and memories.

Every section of our quilt is created differently;
Some bring us happiness while others bring tears
unfortunately.
Some people whom we cherish still love and
support us during these past and future years.
Others for various reasons to us are no longer
near.

Now as you stand back and look at this quilt that
is yours personally;

Remember all the moments both the sad and happy.
They in some form have shaped you and what you have accomplished today;
Both those you like or dislike are part of your future sections in their own way.

Pen Pals

Acquaintances and friendships are made every
day;
Some up close and others a great distance away.
With the single brush of a favorite pen;
We get so excited when letters are received but
also sent.

Most of these people we will never meet in
person;
Distance is the most obvious reason.
But yet with every word we put down on paper;
We get to know one another.

My first pen pal was my beautiful grandmother;
This amazing lady who believed that with the
old-fashioned pen and paper;
We could show others that we cared;
And that is how wonderful acquaintances and
friendships were formed.

Letters can express so many emotions;
Like caring, excitement, joy, sadness, support
and sometimes some personal explosions.
They are a way of special communication;
Also, a unique way of connection.

So to all my amazing pen pals I would like to
say;
I love it when I receive that special letter on any
day.
I look forward to getting to know you better;
and hope to continue doing so many years later.

Words

Everyone has a dream that reminds them of a
special memory.
Sometimes we get that gut instinct to reach out
to a friend or family.
There is nothing wrong if with a text or message
we reach out to somebody;
Saying "hello", "I love you" and "how are you"
should be done regularly.

Saying the three words I love you;
Should be a very natural thing to do.
Giving a hug while we are saying hello or
goodbye;
Should be done routinely and without feeling
shy.

Yet of these things we tend to have second
doubts;
That the other person will rejects us or wonder if
we are totally burnt out.
Sometimes a person is just naturally the touchy
and lovey kind;
And they just want to let you know how special,
loved, cherished , appreciated and that you are
on their mind.

So I have decided to start today;
Dear family and friends by sending some love
your way.
I do hope you get hugged many times during the
day;
And that you continue sharing your love in your
own unique ways.

Our Angels

When our loved ones from us physically part;
With them goes a little piece of our hearts.
Saying goodbye is never easy;
Knowing we won't be seeing them regularly.

There are no words to completely explain;
How we feel or that can take away the pain.
And along with their friends and other family
members;
Having them close to us is all we want to
remember.

We will always cherish our time with them and
those special memories;
Our love for them, in our hearts we will always
carry.
When our special angels reach heaven;
Little pieces of us to that special place are also
given.

While we try to make sense of what happened
and are grieving;
With other loved ones these special angels are
reuniting.

All of them are looking down at us and their
love are sending;
Letting us know that over us they are watching.

So next time you see a beautiful butterfly;
Or maybe a dime on the floor that you almost
walked by.
Yet again you might feel a presence near you;
Remember those are signs that your loved ones
are there too.

Unexpected Journey

This unexpected journey;
is tough on everyone for different reasons
personally.
And yes a lot of us will break down
occasionally;
since there is only so much we can take
emotionally.

I see a lot of posts that just talk negatively;
those are so frustrating to me.
I do understand that everyone is scared;
but please let's try to show understanding to
others cause they are probably also drained.

Now I was reminded recently;
Sometimes we don't know all the facts of the
decisions people take personally.
So I have decided to look at things a bit
differently;
And try to add to the situation a little positivity.

Okay don't get me wrong I know it won't be
easy;

And like everyone I will have days where I am
negative when things seem to go wrong
completely.
But with the support of friends and family;
We can all get through this situation that is scary.

Gazing

As I was gazing out of the window yesterday
morning;
After enjoying my short walk to work even
though it was raining.
I listened to the silence that was in the entire
building;
And thought of how in just a few hours full of
voices it would be bursting.

I have been blessed to work in both domains;
And I have many happy memories that will
forever remain.
Since I work with two amazing groups of
coworkers;
My days are always filled with laughter.

There are times when you wish you could talk to
your family;
But since you are at work they can't be there for
you unfortunately.
It helps when you have great coworkers with
whom you could talk freely;
And as they know and understand your work it
also makes it more easy.

Yes I have been blessed with coworkers who
have turned into friends;
On whom I know I can depend.
I know I can pour my heart out when I have a
breakdown;
And they will listen and be around while I try to
remain strong.

If you are lucky enough like me;
To have a group of coworkers, or maybe it's
volunteer work or a hobby;
Anyone with whom you share most of your
days;
Make sure you laugh and make memories that
will stay.

Real Me

Special bonds are formed every day.
Some you seek and some just come your way.
Some are here for a while and then go away;
Others you know will always stay.

Some pretend to like you;
And it really hurts when you find out the truth.
It can also make you very wary;
And trusting anyone can be very scary.

So when someone approaches you;
And of their intentions you really don't have a
clue;
Just listen what is in your heart;
To any relationship it is always a good start.

And if you happen to find yourself very lucky;
To have someone who is there without any
charge, for free;
Someone who will love and support you without
any reservations;
Please don't use them for your bad intentions.

You may find them annoying;
And find any excuse to do some avoiding.

To them that you can be very hurtful;
And of your actions you must be very careful.

They stay in contact because they love you;
And of all the memories and adventures you
have been through;
But there will come a fateful day;
When they will make the decision to stay away.

It won't be because they no longer love you;
But because of what exists between you two;
Is no longer real, it is a fake;
And the hurtful feelings they can longer take.

So remember that for every action;
There will be some kind of reaction.
It is time for you to decide;
If you will let this special bond slide.

So when you have that once in a lifetime
relationship;
Or that "I must tell you something" friendship;
Please consider yourself very lucky;
Because you are special to somebody.

I am happy that I am able everyday;
To enjoy those kind of relationships and to say;
To those who are very special to me;

That I am blessed to have them as a friend or
family.

They accept the real me;
And don't run away when I act silly.
These special bonds are really precious;
And should be treated as a treasure to us.

Unpredictable

Life and nature share some of the same
characteristics;
Sometimes it is unpredictable and we don't feel
very optimistic.
It feels like it's always rough and we find it
scary;
Our lifeboats and skills don't seem sufficient
enough to protect us fully.

As we are going through these days wondering;
It to our normal lives we will be returning.
We are missing our loved ones dearly;
Missing their hugs, smiles that make us feel
loved completely.

During these times we can take the time to do a
little soul searching;
See if there is something in our current
situations that needs a little tweaking.
Maybe there is a little something about ourselves
we want to improve;
An old habit or flaw that we want to remove.

Everyone at one time or another in their journey;

Has wanted to change paths than the one they
are travelling on currently.
Well now is the time to do some deep
meditating;
And to find what makes us truly happy and is
fulfilling.

When we return to smooth, calm waters once
again;
Reunited with all of our family and friends;
We will cherish all of our current blessings;
And look at what surrounds us with a new
profound understanding

No guarantee

There is no guarantee in life unfortunately;
All we know is that it will go by quickly.
So make sure to enjoy every moment;
And to celebrate every big or small event.

We never know when someone we love will
suffer a casualty.
Or maybe need some form of surgery.
There are others who will feel life is a heavy
burden.
And feel they are in a tornado they keep being
tossed in.

Yes life can feel like we are in quicksand;
And in those times we really need a helping
hand.
To try to pull ourselves out of that sinking
feeling;
And to make the best of the situations we keep
experiencing.

It will be hard to see those we love.
Suffer any of these consequences described
above.
And yes we will feel completely helpless;

And feel other feelings that will leave us
completely breathless.

So while you can enjoy the time you have with
your friends and family;
And make sure they know that without them
your life and heart would feel so empty.
And when life throws something scary their or
your own way;
Make sure they know your love and support is
there to stay.

You must always remember;
That you have more strength when you stick
together.
And that the greatest gift and healing power that
was given to us;
Is the love of our family and friends but also
their support, trust.

Being a Mother

Being a mother is the most important job a
woman will enjoy in many special ways.
Being a mother is also sometimes the most
frightening job you will experience some days.
If you ask everyone how to describe their love
and experiences;
You will get accounts that are both very similar
and very difficult.

It is frightening since you want the best for your
children;
When they get hurt you feel guilty you couldn't
protect them.
Once they grow up and have their own voices;
Even if it's hard you have to step back and let
them make their own choices.

Being a mother is also very rewarding;
And is filled with so many happy blessings.
You will be proud of all of their
accomplishments;
And all the time or conversations you have with
them will be treasured moments.

Being a mother is receiving and early text saying
I love you.
Being a mother is having a child travelling on a
bus to be closer to you.
Being a mother is finding your baskets of
laundry all folded neatly;
And it's knowing your books and scratch tickets
are well stocked since these are you favorite
hobbies.

So today as you are celebrating this very special
day;
Remembering all the special women and men
who have stepped up to fill this role in their own
special ways.
Let's remember all these beautiful memories and
amazing people that are locked away in our
hearts;
Those who are here and especially the ones
whom for different reasons we are apart.

I wish you all a very Happy Mother's Day;
I hope you receive love and new momories in
very special ways.

Success

Success for everyone has a different definition.
And wants to be achieved for many personal
reasons.
For some this has a deep personal meaning;
And for others it has to be done so the ladder
they can keep on climbing.

Well for success is every little thing you can
experience or do;
To make everyone and your surroundings that
are around you;
To be able for a moment to be peaceful and
happy;
And to know they are special to somebody.

It is hearing a child's laughter;
Feeling their arms around my neck as they try
squeezing tighter.
It is knowing that whey they are playing;
They pick up the toy phones and pretend it's you
they are calling.

It is having someone that you can message or
call daily;
And with whom you can cry or act silly.

And it is having those friends with you speak
with only occasionally;
But knowing you can pick up where you left off
easily.

It is having a wonderful husband of many
amazing years;
Who has been with you through great memories
but also is there when you hve meltdowns and
painful tears.
It is having several amazing children that even
though are all grown ups;
Are still taking time to say hi and see what's up.

It is being able to wake up every morning;
And make my way to work walking.
I see so many amazing views on my way;
And it is the perfect start to my day.

It is to be able to work in a field that I enjoy;
And to experience time with great coworkers
and many moments that bring me joy.
It is to be able to continue on with my studies;
Since those have always been a wish for me.

And most of all it is to be surrounded by
amazing friends and family;
Who mean the world to me.

Without their support and love none of this I
would have achieved;
Because surrounded by love makes us complete
I have always believed.

Special

Do you have that special friend or family
member.
With whom you connect to share a bit of
laughter.
Someone who always seems to know when you
are happy or blue;
And seems to suffer or celebrate right along with
you.

I am very lucky along my journey;
That has been both bumpy and joyous for me.
To have met people who have played in my life
a special part;
And they all have a special place in my heart.

I consider myself very fortunate and lucky;
That I can reach out to them just to talk or when
I need somebody.
I hope they all know that I would do the same
for them;
And that I consider them all precious gems.

Whatever the future has in store for me;
I promise to hold on to these ties securely.

I know there was a special reason for us
meeting;
And that is a gift that I will always be
cherishing.

Gesture

Have you even done a kind gesture;
Just to see someone else's pleasure.
When you see their smile so wide;
Your heart swells up with pride.

Have you ever said hi to a stranger;
You should because it makes their day seem
brighter.
Such a simple and kind greeting;
Will have everyone smiling.

Have you told or showed your friends and
family;
That you love them unconditionally.
Do they know how special they are to you;
Or that you appreciate everything they do.

All these little things that should be done
regularly;
Have special meaning and affect others deeply.
Because it's nice and makes up happy;
To know someone cares and loves us tenderly.

Moments

There will be moments when we will never
completely understand.
How a situation got so out of hand.
There will be moments when no matter what
you do;
A person will choose to not like you.

There will be moments;
Where you will think you have more failures
than accomplishments.
And there will be times when your aches and
pains;
Will leave you discouraged and drained.

For all of these things;
We must use our power of understanding.
Only then will we be able analyze and repair
ourselves, relationships or circumstances;
And use a positive attitude to move on and get a
second chance.

We must always remember that as humans we
will hurt and make mistakes.
But it's up to us what actions we take.

We must always remember we are surrounded
by many wonderful blessings;
Such as our family and friends who are on the
same journey we are traveling.

Decisions

In life I have made personal decisions;
That have gotten both good and bad reactions.
And sometimes what could displease somebody;
Is what I need to do to make me happy.

I admit I have made mistakes;
And sometimes there are decisions I would like
to retake.
But I have tried to make sure from my mistakes
I have learned something;
So that next time I wouldn't repeat the same
thing.

During my amazing journey;
I have been blessed with many people who have
supported me.
I wouldn't have gained and succeeded today;
If I didn't have their help and support along the
way.

I have been blessed with an amazing family.
Who through thick and thin have been there for
me.
There are many times I am tired and grumpy;

But they always show love despite that side of
me.

I've been blessed with amazing friends;
Whose support doesn't seem to have an end.
They have endured my many outbursts and
moments of crying;
With phone calls, text messages and their
presence have always been there listening.

I have also have to mention my amazing groups
of coworkers;
Who through the successes and failures always
stick together.
I have received help, support and sometimes a
shake or two during the last seven years;
And I couldn't have asked for a better support
team while I work hard on succeeding.

Like anyone else trying to decide my path hasn't
been easy.
And who knows what will happen next on my
journey.
But I do know I really appreciate my friends,
family and coworkers;
Also appreciate their help, support and love that
always make my life better.

Christmas

Last minute gifts are being readied to get wrapped.
Meals and snacks are being bought and prepared.
With love and laughter, the homes are being filled.
With family, friends most of us are being surrounded.

It is the perfect time to count our blessings.
To remember all the people who made this past year amazing.
Either by being there when we needed love, courage, strength or a boost.
Or by being happy and encouraging when good moments we went through.

During this past year we all went through ups and downs.
We have all worn smiles and sometimes frowns.
We all felt like sometimes we wanted to just quit;
And then had the courage to know if we wanted to succeed, we could do it.

I have discovered new things about myself
recently.
Have knowledge of events and have gained the
love of people that are important to me.
I have learned it is never too late to do some
healing;
And that we should always be prepared to do
some personal growing.

My greatest gifts are my family and friends.
My life would be empty without them.
I just wanted you to all know;
That you all have a special place in my heart that
will always grow.

Merry Christmas everyone.
Hope your celebrations are filled with love and
tons of fun.
I hope you are surrounded by people by whom
you are loved;
And that with new memories you will be
blessed.

www.ingramcontent.com/pod-product-compliance
Lightning Source LLC
Chambersburg PA
CBHW070609160726
48003CB00005B/2184